This Creatures of the World
Series Book belongs to:

Under the Sea, You'll Find Me

is a great book series
to begin your journey of
learning all about
the different types of
animals in the world.

Thank you for your support.

UNDER THE SEA,

Written and Illustrated by

Creatures of the

YOU'LL FIND ME

Lillie Gamez

World Series

To my beautiful children Nezahualcoyotl and Sapphire.
I wish for you to love all of God's creatures
and value life always.

*A special thanks to my mom and dad for always believing in my abilities.
I love you.*

-Lillie

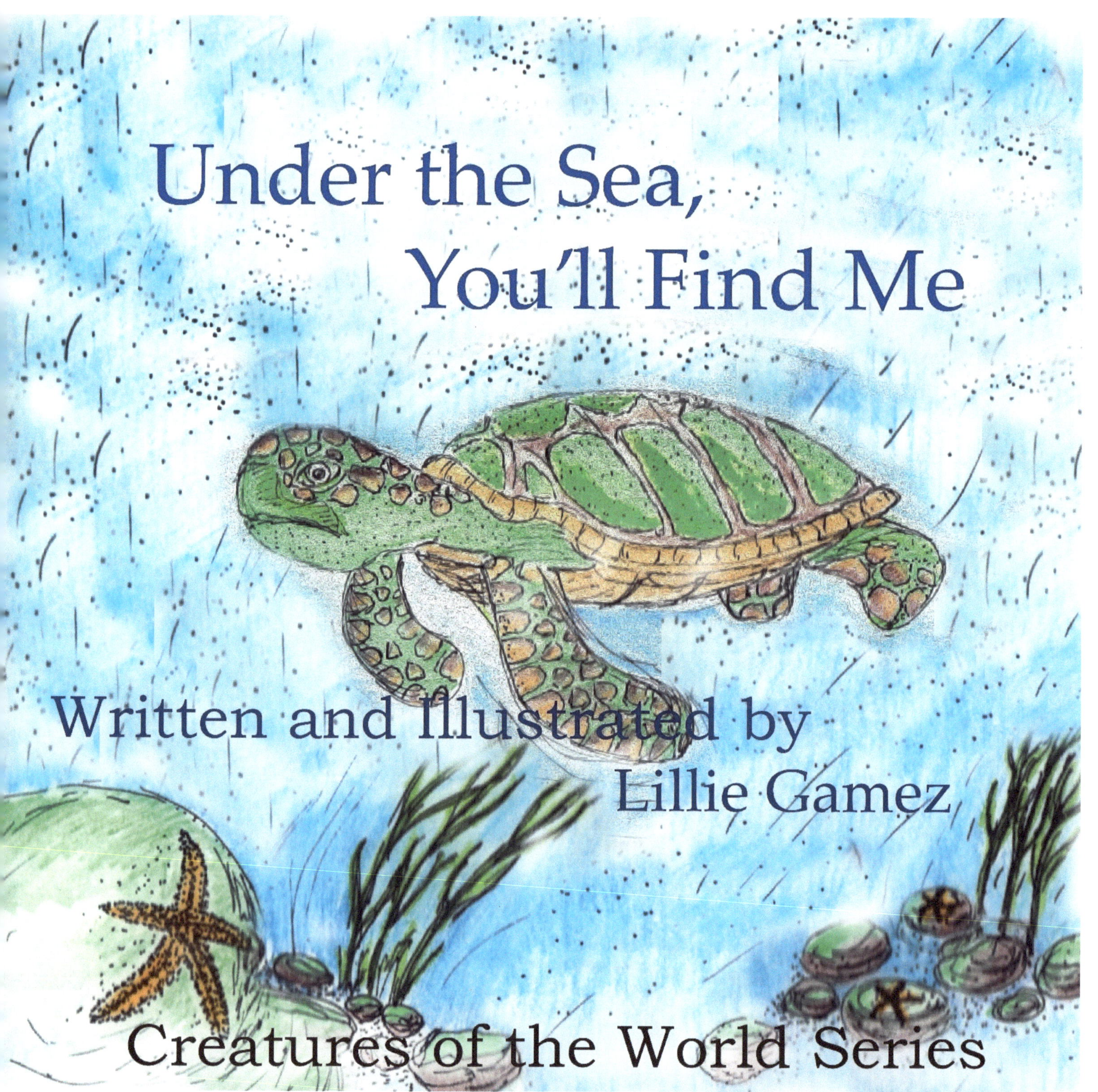

Under the Sea,
You'll Find Me
Written and Illustrated by
Lillie Gamez
Creatures of the World Series

I am Katie the dolphin.
I love to whistle to talk
and flip in the air.

I'm Ted and that is Fred.
We are jellyfish pals.
We love to float
and we gloat as
we glow in the dark.

I'm Ralph the Narwhal
and I have to say
I don't have a horn but a large tooth
springing out of my face.
I use it to swing and sword fight with
my pals in the sea.

I am Sally the Octopus
and you should learn
about me.
I have three hearts to love
and blue blood flows
through me.

I am Randy the Seahorse
in search of a love.
When I find her I will change
colors and we will
dance, dance in the sea.

I am Suki the seal.
I am full of blubber.
I use my whiskers to find
food and I can sleep
underwater.

I am Mike the turtle. I hatched out
of an egg right on the beach.
I crawled into the water before a
bird could get me.

We are called Sea Stars.
We are not fish.
We have no gills,
no scales,
not even fins.

I am a male whale, my
name is Trevor.
I can grow to be about
105 feet long!
I also swallow my food
whole because I don't
have any teeth.

Under the sea, there is so
much to see.
Creatures of all shapes and sizes.
Some big and some tall.
Some wide and some long.

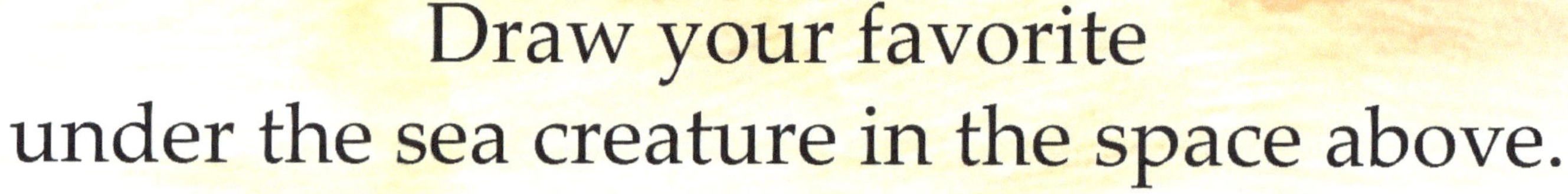

Draw your favorite
under the sea creature in the space above.